NICKY DARE

PANDEMIC
SURVIVAL
How-To Tips & Resources

FROM THE AUTHOR OF "SAFETY & SURVIVAL"

To order additional copies of this book, contact:
Xlibris
1-888-795-4274
www.Xlibris.com
Orders@Xlibris.com

For information contact:
www.NickyDare.com
Education.NickyDare.com

Books are available on paperback and kindle, on Amazon and other participating stores.

Book and cover design by Nicky Dare
Ebook First Edition: March 2020

ISBN: 978-1-7960-9896-9 (sc)
ISBN: 978-1-7960-9897-6 (e)

Print information available on the last page

Rev. date: 04/30/2020

"Preparedness is a 365-day-in-a-year activity. It should be a way of life. Developing a daily routine that reflects this will help you more prepared should an emergency or disaster strike."

Nicky Dare, "Safety and Survival: Personal Preparedness Assessment Guide" page 17

Message From The Author

It is the year 2020. My team and I have just completed our community event in February discussing how to stay prepared for possible next natural and/or manmade disaster. How ironic. *"At the time of disaster, we should not be mobilizing resources, instead we should proactively be prepared already. Preparation ended when a disaster strikes. Our world is changing and it is changing rapidly. We must be able to adapt and sustain ourselves from these changes. ... Culturally, socially, and environmentally..."* Just like many other events I have been advocating in nearly a decade, these words painfully kicked reality. This is what we have now. This unprecedented disaster is what our world is facing.

It is early March 2020. How the world is changing by the minute. We are seeing chaos and panic everywhere around the world, hearing the sad news of how deadly virus has taken many lives. Dow Jones took a free fall on a daily basis, schools were closed, and businesses were directing their employees to work remotely from home. People rushed to buy emergency supplies, while authorities ordered its community to 'shelter in place', to stay home. Disruption to our 'normalcies' just began. What is going to happen? How are we going to survive? When will this end?

Within few days, corona virus 'covid-19' has changed our world of tomorrow completely.

Health care providers, doctors, nurses, medical personnel hastened to be front liners in respond to this unprecedented disaster. We witness heroic efforts of the countless health care workers on the front lines all around the world. Thank you for your dedication and commitment to provide service and utmost care.

Nevertheless, this crisis will get worse before it gets any better.

Now what? We all have a role to play in 'flattening the curve' from spreading by keeping us all lockdown in our home. How long? Few weeks, a month, or maybe for months -- no one knows exactly what to expect ahead. I personally think our goal is not just to 'flattening the curve' but to 'end the spread'.

Around the world, millions are in agony and despair, in fear and are confined at home. How do we overcome these things we have no control of? It is all about the mindset and perspective. Use them wisely.

I am not a scientist nor a pandemic expert, only a human who cares for the safety and wellbeing for others. Preparedness and training for disaster are the bedrocks to survival, both in personal and business. It is the DNA of my organization. So I decided to put together a practical guide for you to provide helpful tools and resources (we all can use these days!) to stay safe and sane during the lockdown at home. Remember, change is constant. Nothing is permanent.

Let's all continue to practice optimism, hope, and kindness. Staying positive and calm are the oxygen to your daily life. So breathe…

We are all in this together.

Nicky Dare

Advocate for Disaster Preparedness

In light of the corona virus 'Covid-19' outbreak, I highly recommend that you check the WHO (World Health Organization) or CDC (Centers for Disease Control and Prevention) websites for the most accurate and latest information.

Disclaimer

This book has been written for information purposes only. Every effort has been made to make this book as complete and accurate as possible. However, there may be mistakes in typography or content. Also, this book provides information only up to the publishing date. Therefore, this book should be used as a guide - not as the ultimate source.

The purpose of this book is to **educate**. The author and the publisher do not warrant that the information contained in this book is fully complete and shall not be responsible for any errors or omissions. The author and publisher shall have neither liability nor responsibility to any person or entity with respect to any loss or damage caused or alleged to be caused directly or indirectly by this book.

TABLE OF CONTENTS

"First off, let's all NOT panic, and stay calm..."

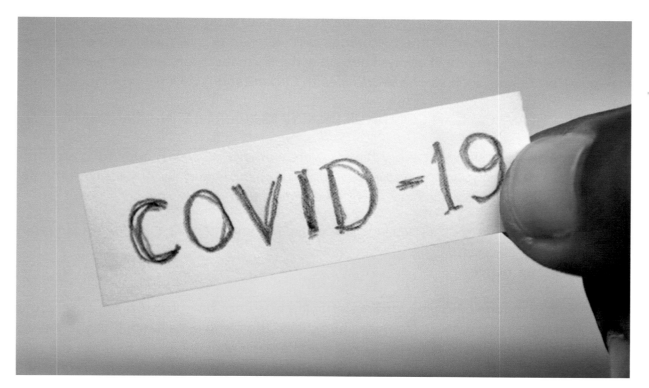

PANDEMIC? IT'S NOT THE END OF THE WORLD

What is a pandemic?

A pandemic is an epidemic of disease that has spread across a large region, for instance multiple continents, or worldwide. (Source: Wikipedia)

Understanding what you need to do during a pandemic will help you realize that pandemic is not the end of the world. You can minimize your stress levels and anxiety by simply **educating** yourself about the pandemic. Know what you need to do once the epidemic starts. Know how to protect yourself as well as your loved ones from getting infected. Know what to buy and practice good personal hygiene, as advised.

Protect your loved ones from panicking if you or a loved one is infected or told to self-isolate. Remember, your kids at home will see and watch what you do and say. We need to continue being the best role model to our kids, especially during a crisis. You can achieve this by being prepared before the pandemic starts and by understanding that you are not the only one affected. Know that countless people are doing the best they can to come up with a solution as well as preventative measures. So, focus on keeping up to date with positive news.

✓ STAY CALM BY FINDING OUT WHAT PROFESSIONALS ARE SAYING

Finding out and understanding what health professionals are saying about a pandemic that has everyone panicking will help you maintain your sanity when everyone else is losing their mind. That is why you must always keep up with information concerning a pandemic only from reputable sources such as *The World Health Organization (WHO)* or your local clinic.

✓ HERE'S HOW YOU CAN CONTINUE ENJOYING YOUR LIFE IN A PANDEMIC

A pandemic is not a sign that everything you are working towards is coming to an end. Its presence does not mean you should stop developing yourself financially, physically, or mentally. You can still enjoy your life while coping with a pandemic.

✓ EFFECTIVE TIPS TO CONTINUE WITH YOUR PROFESSIONAL LIFE FROM HOME

Set up a home office

Advancing or maintaining your professional life does not have to stop because you are home bound during a pandemic. You can still achieve the same excellence that you are well-known for at the office while at home. There are a few things you can do to make the home environment conducive to office work. Setting up a home office is a great place to start. Make sure your home office is as tidy as the office you usually use.

If possible, you can even dress formally to give yourself and everyone around the house the sense of how important your office hours are. Allocate 6 to 8 hours to continuing with your work and do not allow any interruptions. Make sure your home office resembles your regular office where possible.

Talk to your loved ones about the need for quiet hours

Working from home has many advantages, including controlling your schedule, working in your terms as well as maximizing on time otherwise wasted traveling to the office. Nonetheless, working from home comes with its share of disadvantages, such as constant interruptions as well as noise. Therefore, talking to your loved ones about the need for quiet hours free from interruptions is essential.

Make sure everyone understands that you will not tolerate any disturbances unless there is an emergency. In this way, you will be able to concentrate better, and it will show in the quality of the work that you produce. That is how you can continue enjoying your work in a pandemic.

Understand working from home is as crucial as working from the office

The quality of your work is determined by how you approach the work you do. If you treat working from home differently from working from the office, the quality of your work will show. Avoid producing below standard practice by carrying out work you do from home the same way you handle work from the office.

Keep in mind that all that matters is that you are producing quality work. Stay in touch with your supervisor and your colleagues if you are working on a project that requires communication.

✓ DIFFERENT WAYS OF DEVELOPING YOUR RELATIONSHIPS IN A PANDEMIC

Stay in touch

Staying in touch with your loved ones during a pandemic is vital to keep your relationships healthy.

Help each other out around the house

If you are required to remain indoors for a certain period, you can continue growing your relationships with the people you live with by helping each other out. Assisting with household chores and taking turns minding the kids or pets can help strengthen your relationship. It is also a great way of distracting yourself from the bad news circulating.

Work on assignments with your co-workers or classmates

If you are a student, you can continue working on your assignments with other students online. If you are a working adult, you can keep with your projects or work assignments with other co-workers online. Sharing ideas, correcting each other, and coming up with new methods of tackling your work becomes more comfortable and even faster.

Chapter 2

How to overcome anxiety during a Pandemic

A pandemic is not something that happens frequently but whenever it happens the ramifications can be brutal. One common effect affecting a majority of people during a global outbreak is anxiety.

- *Are you experiencing pandemic uneasiness?*
- *Do you feel uneasy about the future post the pandemic?*
- *Do you worry if you and the people you care about will survive or not?*

If you answered "yes" to any of the questions, you may be experiencing anxiety and that is normal! Worrying is a normal response to a crisis like a worldwide virus outbreak. However, some people worry much more than others and as such, may potentially become a problem which can affect their wellbeing if not properly dealt with.

The good news is that there are many ways of managing and overcoming anxiety in difficult situations. The goal is to maintain your mental health even in the most trying circumstances so you can come out on the other side ready to pick up your life and continue being great.

"Mindset is the best secret weapon in facing fear.
It is a way of thinking."
Nicky Dare, Advocate to Safety and Survival

To help you, here are some steps to take in order to overcome anxiety during a pandemic:

1. Accepting that there are certain things you can change and others that you can not
In every situation, there are things that you can change and things you simply cannot change. Acceptance is the first step when dealing with anxiety. Accept that there are things that are beyond your control and influence. Accept that there are things that you can influence. Leave the things that you cannot control to those who can and focus on the things that are within your control.

By being realistic and focusing on the things you can control, you will be able to focus all your energy into things that will give you results instead of things that will waste your efforts and cause you more worry and stress.

Letting go is the most important step of dealing with anxiety, however, it is probably the most difficult to take. You just have to keep trying until you get it right. It takes some practice.

2. Stay in touch with people close to you and the rest of the world
During a pandemic lockdown, people are asked to remain indoors and refrain from their usual activities that include social events and gatherings. Now humans are designed in such a way that they need social contact in order to live a healthy life. When you are on

lockdown and facing recurrent episodes of anxiety you have to boost your contact with other people. Stay connected and talk more, especially to people with a positive attitude.

When you are on lockdown you are prohibited from physical contact and interactions, but you are not prohibited from texting, phone calls, and video chats. So, if you are experiencing worry and overwhelming feelings of despair, pick up the phone and chat up some of your family members and friends.

You should be careful though on the type of people that you connect with. Staying connected with the right persons will help in maintaining a positive outlook on things. Connecting with pessimistic and negative people, on the other hand, will only worsen any existing anxiety.

3. Try to get out of your head by helping others

Sometimes you can get rid of feelings of doom and worry by helping others. In times of a crisis, there are always many people in need of assistance. These could be the elderly, daycare schools for personnel actively involved in a crisis, volunteering in crisis management centers, homeless people, etc.

Helping people in need can give you a great sense of satisfaction and usefulness. It can occupy your time that you would have otherwise used for dark thoughts of doom. It is the perfect way to use your time and forget about your worries.

Try to partake a 30-day challenge to stay connected virtually during the lockdown, an awareness initiated by iDAREcares.org with its goal to save lives. Learn more by visiting their website.

4. Plan your days

For the most part, people who worry and suffer from anxiety during a pandemic are the people who sit around idle. When you have nothing to do you get bored and dwell on your thoughts which fuel anxiety.

The best way to enjoy your days during a lockdown is to plan. Know exactly what you are going to do when. Include a mixture of exciting activities and serious activities. Planning gives your days structure and it is that structure that will help you overcome anxiety.

5. Always keep things in perspective

Keeping things in perspective is another recommended way of getting through a crisis like a pandemic. If you get the feeling that things will not get better try to look at the other scale of things as well, the other scale says things will get better. If your mind says you are not going to make it, listen to the other part of your mind that says, of course, you will make it.

6. Be careful on the internet

The internet is the gasoline of negative vibrations and feelings of doom. You may go online with the intention of getting news update, but you can quickly find yourself down a rabbit hole of pessimistic posts and comments. These types of posts and comments can lead you down a very dark path that can be difficult to recover from.

It is important to stay informed, but it is more important to watch your steps on the internet. That is how you overcome anxiety linked to worldwide disasters like a virus pandemic. In fact, prelude to this outbreak I was in the process of launching my next book called "Unplug" digital detox (how ironic!) and had to put this aside for now, rather I decided to launch this relevant guide.

7. Finally, know when to seek help

Anxiety is a well-known mental condition. In some people, it can easily become a disorder that can cause more damage than you might think. There are signs that you should keep an eye out for and seek help when you notice them.

If you are becoming very irritable, overloaded with negative thoughts, unable to focus on anything and feeling completely hopeless, it is time to seek help. You can talk to someone you trust to get some help if you live alone or do not have anyone you can trust that way you should call a healthcare practitioner without delay.

Chapter 3

How to reassure your kids during a Pandemic

During a pandemic, the lives of many people are disrupted, and people of all age groups felt the effects, kids included. As a parent or guardian, you have to make sure your kids are alright. Making sure that your kids are alright goes further than just protecting them from contamination, you have to ensure that they have a peace of mind as well.

In times of a crisis, kids become uneasy and get stressed, too, especially if they do not fully understand what is happening. It is, therefore, essential to reassure your kids during a pandemic.

1. Deal with your issues and control your anxiety first

If you have ever been on a flight, you may have noticed that the safety instructions always say put your mask and life jacket first before helping children. There is a reason for that: you can run out of air or drown before you can finish helping your kids, putting at risk not only your life but also that of your kids.

Likewise, before you can assist your children wrap their heads around a pandemic, you need to gain control of your issues first. Kids can pick up and adopt the negative energy coming from their parents. If you feel anxious because of the pandemic, they too will share that anxiety.

Whatever emotions or energy you exude, your children can pick up on it as well, and it can affect them profoundly. So, work on your anxiety and deal with other emotions you may have about the pandemic. There are some ways of dealing with anxiety during an epidemic, look it up and help yourself first. Once you have helped yourself, you can then go ahead and help your children.

2. Educate yourself on the subject before talking to your kids

To reassure kids, you need to make them understand the situation. Take time to educate yourself about the pandemic. Read reputable and reliable websites like the WHO or following simplified courses about the pandemic in question. Anticipate questions that your kids might ask and look for the answers in advance. When you have acquired enough knowledge, you can then engage your kids.

3. Talk to your kids

You must know what your kids are thinking and how they feel about the whole crisis. To do so, you need to communicate with them. Gather your kids around and calmly explain what a pandemic is and what is causing it.

Explain to them how it can be stopped and make sure to use past pandemics as an example that pandemics can end. Let them ask any questions they may have on the subject and give them honest and truthful answers. If they ask something you do not know, let them know that you are going to find out and get back to them.

Take note of their fears and worries and explain to them why you think they should not worry. The idea is to make sure your kids know why specific measures are in place and that it will not last forever.

4. Update your kids

Keeping your kids informed is part of the reassuring process. Every day make sure you update the kids on the situation. Even if things are not any better than the previous day, you should just go ahead and update them. The information is received and processed better when it is coming from you than when they come across it on the internet.

5. Allow room for your kids to stay in touch with friends and family

If the pandemic requires people to stay indoors and not get outside the house, you should put some structures in place for your kids to stay connected to their friends and other members of the family.

Allow them the use of the internet and a phone where they can keep in touch with their friends at least once a day. This way they will know and be assured that the other people they care about are also fine and keeping well.

6. Make your kids feel safe

You should strive to make your kids feel safe. Cultivate a positivity culture and never stop letting them know that the pandemic is passing by, and everything will be fine. Make them understand that even if they were to get infected, you would be there to ensure that they are cared for and nursed back to health. Simply put, remove fear and worry from your household and replace them with optimism and hope.

7. If contact must be avoided with their grandparents

Elderly can sometimes be more prone to infections during a pandemic. It is therefore essential that physical contact between kids and their grandparents be avoided. Although this may have an impact on the emotional wellbeing of the children, it is important that the grandparents or the parents explain to the children the reasons for such actions.

If explained properly, the kids will understand. Something along these lines should work out well: *"Grandpapa and Grandma need to stay away from you for a while because need to take care of our health. We can still talk on the phone or video-chat. They still love you very much and will miss you!"*

Chapter 4

Reconnecting with family members during a pandemic

During a pandemic, some people have no option but to self-isolate and others are put into quarantine to get better control of the disease and stop its spread. These extreme measures can put a strain on some relationships, especially closely-knit families who see each other often and do things together. In some cases, a parent has to be isolated from their kids, and that can profoundly affect parent-child relationships.

Staying connected during a pandemic is very important for families. By just practicing a few habits, you and your family can come out of a pandemic even stronger than before. Here are some practical ways to encourage you stay connected with your family when self-isolating:

Talk about the situation

Talking is the healthiest way of dealing with any issues related to emotions. If you want your relationships to survive a pandemic lockdown or to repair fractured relations, you have to take some time to talk to your loved ones. Talk about the disease and why it is essential to maintain a period of isolation. Go on to discuss in detail how the separation will go and what methods of communication you will adopt to stay in touch. Make it a must to give each other regular updates until the period of isolation is over.

Check-in with texts and video calls

Check on your loved ones through regular texts and video calls. We live in the technology era, which makes it possible to remain connected with people regardless of the distance. It is even possible to have group calls where the whole family can participate in different locations.

Play online games together

Staying connected with family does not mean talking and chatting alone. You have to incorporate other activities that you can do together. Playing games online, together as a family, can maintain the connection needed to get through a lockdown with minimum damage. There are different kinds of games online to suit various family interests. Depending on the sort of things you like as a family, you can play board games, sports games, role play, strategy, adventure, etc.

Work on a family project from a distance

Another way to reconnect with family members is to start a family project. A family project will ensure that you frequently communicate as a family. It will also bring about some challenges that you will have to work together to overcome, thereby uniting the family. The family project does not have to be complicated; it could be starting a family YouTube channel, blogging, or business. You could also start preparing the family's genealogical tree.

Plan a future family get-together or vacation

While you are in self-isolation or lockdown, try to work together as a family to plan the next gathering or family vacation. You can give each other tasks to do and make decisions together until the whole plan comes along. Planning together gives family members the feeling of being loved and being relevant, which plays a significant role in building connections and reconnecting for those who had lost touch.

Help each other with goals and resolutions

Encourage each other in coming up with goals and resolutions. Discuss and establish each other's vision board and come up with a mutual vision board as a family. Help each other evaluate past achievements and failures and map up new objectives for when the pandemic is over. By being involved in each other's lives, you build a stronger bond, guaranteed to withstand any crisis that may threaten to shake your walls.

Time to forgive and reunite

A time of crisis is an excellent opportunity to tackle past hurts. Talk about these issues openly with the relevant family member and forgive or ask forgiveness where necessary. Paradoxical, though it may seem, a pandemic is an opportune moment to mend and start over any broken or wounded relationship with other family members. It may hurt at first, when dealing with these issues, especially if there were deeply buried emotions, but the intense feeling of relief and restoration will be liberating once relationships are mended. This is the best time to practice letting go and rekindle, reinstall the core of family values: unconditional love.

Chapter 5

How to stay calm in the midst of chaos?

One of the main reasons why most people panic during times of uncertainty is because they pay too much attention to rumors, misinformation as well as being under informed. A pandemic is one of the many reasons people get caught up in a frenzy.

One good example is global crisis with the Corona virus that started in December 2019. Before even the corona virus was declared a pandemic, the whole world was stuck in the midst of uncertainty, stock markets crashed, fear led to a panic buying.

The normal response when something you do not have control over strikes is to panic. You get caught up in the fear of the pandemic affecting your region and start losing your grip on reality. The people who have the ability to keep calm in the midst of chaos tend to survive the craziness better than others. It all begins by listening before acting. Listen to expert advice, listen to verified news, and most importantly, learn to filter what you hear.

Things you can do to remain calm during a global outbreak:

1. Do your research

One of the main reasons people battle with stress and anxiety during a period of uncertainty comes from being under informed. Doing proper research will help you stay calm while everyone else is losing their grip on reality.

A few ways you can be sure you have done proper research and are well informed is by paying attention to your sources of information. For example, you can try sticking to reputable sources for up to date information concerning the pandemic. Only listen to professional advice when it comes to implementing precautionary measures.

2. Take professional advice seriously

Most people may be infected simply because they are failing to take professional advice seriously. For example, if you are advised by experts to self-isolate or make use of certain sanitary products make sure you do just that.

Avoid taking things lightly. If you are advised to stay calm and avoid panic buying, make sure that is precisely what you do. There is always a good reason why professionals give the kind of advice they give with regards to their trade, particularly in dire conditions. Health professionals are not an exception.

3. Avoid panic buying

Hold up wait, what is up with all that hoarding of essential items at the beginning of this outbreak? C'mon, TPs? Seriously? I am still unglued of all that panic reaction. Okay, moving on. Panic buying comes from paying attention to false rumors. That is why it is important to be selective when it comes to your sources of information concerning the pandemic. There are many reasons why you should avoid panic buying. One good and humane example is that of taking into consideration the rest of the population.

Keep in mind that there are a lot of people who are also affected by the pandemic and are in equal need of the same products as you. Another reason is that you may panic buy a lot of things that you won't really need and as a result strain your finances and prevent access to others who may have a greater need of such articles.

4. Talk about something else

One way of ensuring your mind believes what you want it to believe is by dwelling on one subject over and over again. Talking about a bad event repeatedly and focusing on the number of affections and the consequences of the event only increases your stress levels.

One effective method of staying calm during a tragic event is by finding something else to talk about. Concentrate more on positive subjects that boost morale.

This does not mean you should ignore the fact that there is a crisis because that is impossible. You can stay up to date with the relevant information, however, do not overdo it.

You can allocate a few minutes a day to check on the latest headlines concerning the crisis and no more. You can check the news first thing in the morning and a few minutes during the day or in the evening. Make sure you concentrate on doing other activities afterward.

5. Make time for morale boosting activities

The stress and anxiety that you battle with in a crisis like a pandemic can lead to certain illnesses that can be easily avoided. Impossible as it may be to believe, the stress and anxiety that you have because of the crisis is something that can be controlled. You can achieve this by intentionally setting aside fun or morale boosting activities that you and the rest of the family can do every day.

One good example is playing a game that everyone loves and sticking to it for considerable hours. You can also focus on practicing effective ways of continuing with your work if you are advised to work from home. Instead of dwelling on the fact that you are no longer able to go to the office you can focus on the many advantages that come with working from home.

CHAPTER 6

How to stay focused when working from home

Most people who have attempted working from home have found out one thing: It is hard to get things done at home! The people who have persisted with a home-office environment have gone on to find something else: working from home can be highly productive if you go about it the right way.

Working from home requires an ability to manage distractions and maintain focus. It can be hard during the first days, but if you remain structured, it will grow on you, and you will be able to produce results.

Some situations require that you work from home- Your child falling sick on a last-minute, with no one to look after her; the office space is undergoing repairs or improvements; or a general lockdown where no one is allowed to leave their homes.

Whatever your reason for working from home, here are some tips to help you remain productive:

1. Take some time to create a working area
You cannot just take your computer and sit on your bed. If you want to be productive while working from home, you need to prepare a proper workspace and create an ideal environment for productivity.

Preferably it should be away from your bedroom because that is a place you mostly associate with rest.

If you have other people around the house, you should consider picking a place that they won't need as much while you are working. For most people, the kitchen or dining is the most logical place as it can leave the living room for the rest of the family.

When you have picked your working area, make sure you install everything you need to achieve your tasks. Some things you would most probably require include stationery, a power source, a comfortable chair, a phone, and a good background for video calls.

2. **Plan your tasks and schedule**

Let's be honest- if you are working from home, you will not work the same schedule as at the office. For starters, you won't have to worry about the time spent for commuting, you won't have to worry about where to go for lunch, and most importantly you won't have colleagues coming to you with different agendas. That means you gain a lot of time, and if you plan well, you can be very productive and left with extra time for yourself without affecting your tasks. So, plan what you need to do and when you need to do it.

Do not forget to prioritize when you are planning. Unlike at the office where your manager or assistant prioritizes your work for you, at home, you should take care of that yourself. Make sure you put all of the essential tasks early in the morning before everyone is up. Push conference calls towards midday and then place the less

critical stuff late afternoon. This way, you will be able to complete the essential tasks while you are still fresh and full of energy in the morning.

3. **Dress for work**

This one needs to be said: Get rid of your pajamas or "home clothes"! Your body and mind associate your home clothes with rest. You may experience focus issues if you attempt to work from home in your home clothes. So, wake up, shower and dress as if you are going to the actual office. Dressing up can also boost your self-confidence and stature, improving your productivity and creativity.

4. **Remember to report back to your manager frequently**

Maintaining structure is what gets things done when working from home. There is nothing that gives you more structure than reporting what you do and getting feedback. When you are working from home, try to report on your tasks as frequently as possible. It will boost your productivity.

5. **Take regular breaks**

It is important to take regular short breaks to avoid straining. Taking 5 to 10 minutes break to talk to members of the family or getting involved in a short activity with them will great help to refocus and re-energize after the break.

6. **Avoid Distraction**

Television is the number 1 enemy of productivity. Avoid keeping the television on while working. You must be ruthless with this rule! You can however use this to your advantage.

Set a goal to watch your favorite series or documentary once a specific task of your work is completed. On-demand tv and recording is widely accessible nowadays- so make the most of these facilities. Treat yourself with your favorite show once done with your work. This could be an effective incentive to your work.

CHAPTER 7

How to stay healthy while you are stuck at home

Being on lockdown during a pandemic should not be an excuse to let go of your body and engage in an unhealthy lifestyle. If you have to stay indoors longer than usual, it is even more essential to adopt a healthy lifestyle. In that way, you can avoid putting yourself at risk for certain conditions linked to unhealthy living. By staying on top of your behavior when you are stuck at home, you can prevent yourself from developing things like diabetes, high blood pressure, obesity, and muscle atrophy. Studies have shown that people who do not maintain a healthy lifestyle when stuck at home often find it difficult to resume normal activities after the home period is over. Going back to work may prove challenging. So if you are going to be held at home, for whatever reason, here are some tips to help you stay healthy:

1. Eat healthily

You would think that this tip does not require mentioning, but you will be surprised at the things people eat when they are stuck at home. It's fine to eat junk food once in a while, but going on a junk food bender during a lockdown can cause you many issues. So take some time and plan out your meals and snacks. For every 90% of whole, healthy foods, you can reward yourself with 10% of feel-good fare.

2. Get physical

Most people mistake physical exercise for body looks. It's much more than that, exercise helps the body release stress, clear the mind, and it is good for the heart as it gets the blood flowing. When you are stuck at home, exercising can boost your sense of wellbeing and prevent you from suffering from dangerous health conditions like depression and anxiety.

3. Read books

With online streaming sites being so popular, it is easy to get stuck on the couch and binge-watch tv shows. However, people tend to forget the negative impact of long hours watching tv on the eyes, back, and intellect. In order to stay healthy when you are stuck indoors try and incorporate some books in between your tv shows. Taking time off the screen and moving images can do you a lot of good in as far as your eyes are concerned. Audiobooks can also help with the advantage of doing another activity while listening to the book.

4. Feed the mind

Maintaining some level of intellect is another way of staying healthy when stuck at home. There are many ways of keeping your brain active during a lockdown. You could play strategy and logic games that require you to think. You could also enroll in an online course or join forums that discuss highly intellectual topics.

5. Take care of your mental health

When one is stuck indoors, they risk developing mental health issues, especially if they are alone. Taking care of your mental health is an absolute priority when you are locked down. You need to maintain contact with friends and family if you are going to be stuck indoors for a long time. You do not necessarily need it to be physical contact, video chats, texting, and phone calls can do just fine.

6. Find a project

Having a sense of purpose can play a crucial role in maintaining a healthy attitude when stuck at home. It does not even have to be a big project. Just a simple project with results can work wonders. You can embark on a simple project like redecorating your room or something a bit more challenging, like DIY (Do-It-Yourself) projects.

7. Improve yourself

When you are stuck at home, you could use that time to improve yourself. Learn a new skill that will help you get ahead when you eventually return to the world. Educating yourself will remove the unhealthy feeling of being "stuck" and replace it with feelings of finding a new purpose.

8. Help others

Being helpful to other people while you are stuck at home can do wonders for your mental health. There are many ways of helping other people that you can try. One example would be to help older people do online shopping. Another example would be to take some time to listen to other people's problems (although not too much to avoid being depressed yourself). You can dispense services directly linked to your profession, which can also help you stay fresh and sharp for when you eventually return to your work.

9. Explore and expand your horizons

It is always healthy to explore and expand one's horizons. The world has so much more to offer than what you already know or think. So when stuck at home, take time to explore other cultures, try new foods, and above all, make sure you come out on the other side a better and stronger person.

10. Do not miss your medical consultations

Lastly, if you have medical conditions or scheduled checkups, do not pass upon them. Instead, use technology to turn up for your medical appointments and consultations. If you have prescriptions to renew, you can also do that using telemedicine platforms and other technology.

Chapter 8

How to kick viruses and allergies out of your life

Viruses and allergies are a reason for concern for most people. Infections spread through personal contact from one infected person to another as well through the air. If you are continually battling with allergies or live with someone who is, then you know how annoying viruses and allergies can be. Luckily you can reduce the impact that they have and get rid of them by controlling your environment.

1. Clean frequently

Continually cleaning your house as well as frequently touched surfaces with a disinfectant will help get rid of dust, pollen, and other allergy triggers. Make sure you allow the cleaned surfaces to air dry for the best disinfection. Use a damp cloth when cleaning to trap allergens. Getting rid of clutter can stop your allergies from worsening and viruses from spreading. Therefore, make sure your house remains tidy and always wear a mask when cleaning.

Wash your sheets in hot water at least once a week and keep your bathroom clean and free of mold. Get rid of carpets and rugs because they can trap allergens. You can buy smaller rugs that are washable and dry up quickly. Scented detergents and cleaners can also trigger allergies, so stick to using fragrance-free products.

2. Use air filters

Air HEPA filters and other purifiers help remove allergens from the air inside your house. They can be installed in your air-conditioning system or your ventilation system. Using HEPA filters can help in getting rid of pollen, pet dander, dust mites, smoke, and bacteria.

3. Know your triggers

Knowing your triggers can help you cope with allergies as well. You can lessen your allergy symptoms by reducing your exposure to specific triggers as well as avoiding them. If you are not yet sure about what you are allergic to, you can carry out allergy tests. Ask your health advisor about the best allergy tests for diagnosing your symptoms.

Skin prick tests are one of the most common tests allergists perform. Your allergist injects tiny amounts of common allergens to see if they provoke a reaction.

4. Allergy-proof your home

Keeping your home free from allergy-triggers or viruses also includes using bedding materials that are a barrier against allergens, for instance, hypoallergenic bedding. Use hypoallergenic pillows and comforters to control allergies or reduce your allergy symptoms.

Avoid upholstered furniture and stick to metallic and wooden furniture. Keep your kitchen sink mold-free and scrub daily. Scrub and towel-dry the tub and shower area daily. Remove moldy shower curtains and keep your bathroom mats clean. Always fix leakages around the house.

Plants grown inside the house can also act as allergy triggers by collecting dust mites and mold spores. Get rid of dried house plants and reduce the number of plants you keep inside the house. Make sure you get rid of food leftovers and garbage as well.

5. Try home remedies

You can also try reducing allergies by making use of home remedies such as bromelain, quercetin, and essential oils. Bromelain is effective at preventing allergies, and it works by improving breathing and reducing swelling.

Bromelain can be obtained in Pineapples. Quercetin aids in controlling your allergy symptoms by stabilizing the release of histamines. Histamine levels can also be reduced by taking 2 000 milligrams of vitamin C every day. Quercetin can be found in citrus fruits, broccoli, and green tea. Oils such as eucalyptus essential oil and peppermint essential oil can also help treat or reduce symptoms.

The anti-inflammatory effects that peppermint essential oil has can help reduce bronchial asthma. Eucalyptus oil works more effectively when added to your washing or laundry during allergy season.

6. Avoid physical contact

Stop the spread of viruses by avoiding physical contact. If you are the one infected, make sure you use napkins or tissues when sneezing or coughing. Keep a reasonable distance between yourself and other non-infected people. Make sure you avoid shaking hands, constantly touching your face, nose, and mouth to prevent spreading the virus.

7. Practice social distancing

Social distancing is an excellent way of controlling or slowing down the spread of a rapidly spreading disease. Practicing social distancing is a unique way of protecting yourself and other people.

8. Boost your immune system

Your immune system is an incredible machine programmed to protect your body from foreign agents like viruses, bacteria, allergens. There are several ways of boosting your immune system, which range from taking supplements to having the right diet and maintaining healthy hygiene- avoiding smoking and drinking alcohol in moderation and exercising regularly.

9. Treat your allergies before your symptoms begin

You can reduce your allergy symptoms by using allergy shots. A health professional gives allergy shot at frequent intervals over three to five years. However, you will be receiving an injection twice

a week in the first few months. You will then be required to go for treatment every few weeks according to your doctor's prescription.

Completing your allergy shots treatment can help get rid of your allergies completely. Allergy shots work by numbing you to your allergen source. They can help reduce symptoms such as itchy eyes and a runny nose.

10. Drink lots of water

Adequate hydration is the key to maintaining good health. We cannot overemphasize this fact enough. Drinking lots of water can help in reducing the risks of a viral infection or allergic symptoms. The fluid will help the body drain all toxins, clear up the respiratory passages, drain blocked sinuses, and thin any accumulated mucus.

Chapter 9

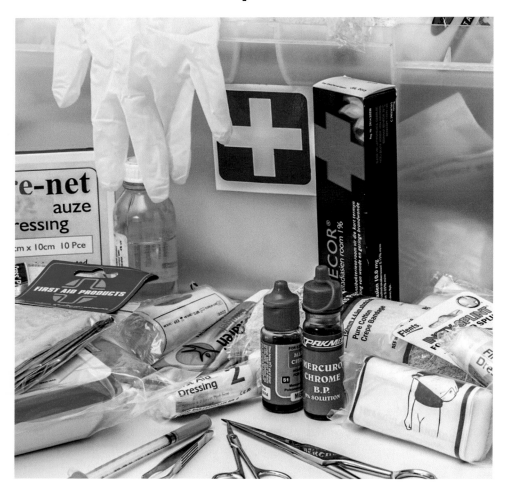

How to get your Pandemic Emergency kits ready

The key to surviving a pandemic with the minimum effect is to be prepared. For over a decade, I have shown different emergency items that needed to be included in your disaster bags for different emergency purposes. It is even more relevant if there is going to be a lockdown.

To prepare for a pandemic and a possible lockdown, you have to put together an emergency kit and store essential supplies.

An emergency kit you should have before an outbreak

Before there is even a worldwide outbreak, you should have the following items in your emergency kit:

Purchase and keep some prescription medication and over the counter medicines. Prescription medication includes any form of medication that you would typically take for your existing condition. Over the counter medicines include analgesics, antiemetic, stomach relievers, antihistamines, vitamins, etc. Take good note of the expiry dates for your medication and make sure to renew it at least 30 days before it expires.

Ask for copies of your medical records from your physician. These can be very useful to first responders in the event of an emergency during a pandemic.

Keep a list of emergency numbers for the different government departments.

Store reasonable quantities of tinned or dry food and bottled water.

Store sanitary and hygiene products.

Have a First-Aid kit readily available- usual antiseptic, bandage, gloves, scissors and plaster bands are essential to attend to any bumps or bruises while confined at home. Household spares and DIY kits can also become handy if you need to replace light bulbs or conduct minor repairs. So, it is always advisable to buy in advance the right type of spare bulbs which you use at home as well as the standard batteries for household equipment. A general DIY toolkit can also be of essential help since hardware stores would most likely be closed during a lockdown.

Refill and update your emergency kit during an outbreak

Once a situation is declared a pandemic, refill and update your emergency kit according to the type of situation. The following items must be checked and be available if possible:

A thermometer to control body temperature. If you live with other people, it is best to get a digital non-contact thermometer. Don't forget to also buy spare batteries for your digital thermometer!

Hand sanitizers and liquid soap are a must.

A backup glucometer to measure blood sugar if you or any member of your family has diabetes.

One-time use only surgical gloves.

Sanitary masks, if agents of the outbreak are transmissible by air or droplets. Pay attention to the health authorities and get the right sanitary masks they recommend.

Food to last you for a week or two. When storing food for a pandemic, always make sure you think of other people as well. Do not overbuy to the extent that you create shortages for other people.

Update and refill your medication. Add other medication that is related to the outbreak as instructed by the authorities.

Ingredients from alternative medication can also be useful during a pandemic. Get lemons, honey, ginger, cinnamon, mint leaves, essential oils, and other natural agents known to have healing or antiseptic properties.

Entertainment material. Depending on your interests and the number of family members, books and magazines are always a good option. Board games and group games, as well as other entertainment activities for multiple people, is also an excellent choice to keep. If you have pets, do not forget to buy pet food.

You should also get some stationery and other office-related supplies just in case you have to self-isolate and work from home.

If you can afford it, an Air-Purifying respirator can be a good and useful investment.

When preparing or refilling your emergency pandemic kit, remember always to check expiration dates for perishable items. Do not also forget to think about other people, meaning DO NOT OVER-BUY.

Please consider to shop your emergency items online, if you haven't done so. And I recommend to assemble emergency items that are approved by FEMA or Red Cross. Please consider to use Smile Amazon where you can shop and Amazon gives to a charity you select. iDARE is a registered nonprofit 501(c) (3) with its mission to save lives by educating and mobilizing resources for disaster risk reduction. Learn more, please visit: www.iDAREcares.org

CHAPTER 9

How past pandemics can prepare businesses to face new ones

The impact that a pandemic has on individuals ***psychologically, socially***, and ***financially*** can be devastating. Understanding past pandemics and their adverse effects on people's lives, as well as the economy, can help us learn from these past events.

You can survive the pandemic by avoiding making the same mistakes made in the past. You can also come out sane by adopting some of the preventative measures taken in the past and adopting the right attitudes and reflexes.

One example of a global pandemic that had devastating impacts on the economy and people's lives, in general, is the 1918 Spanish flu. Many lessons can be drawn from the global pandemic that had severe economic and psychological consequences on businesses and individuals.

What have we learned from the past?

SOME OF THE LESSONS YOU CAN LEARN FROM PAST PANDEMICS

The importance of containment

During a pandemic, the number one priority for health professionals should be controlling the spread of an epidemic. Everyone in the health sector understands this, and that is why there are containment rules in place.

Rules or instructions given should be obeyed to prevent panicking as well as further complications. Staying at home, refraining from certain activities, using certain products, and self-isolating are some of the most important instructions that must be observed.

The main reason why most people died from the 1918 Spanish flu is the same reason that is likely to cause more deaths in any other global pandemic. Many deaths were caused by the virus spreading from people to people in confined spaces or in large gatherings.

This mainly happens because people refuse to avoid large gatherings, and they also refuse to self-quarantine properly.

The need for businesses to prepare for the impact of the pandemic

The consequences that the Spanish flu had included labor shortages and increased rates of physical disability, among other things. Most effects rose from the panic surrounding the virus. The panicking also worsened as businesses were temporarily closed, public gatherings banned, and sporting events canceled. Luckily, we can avoid going down the same route and facing similar consequences. Knowing and preparing for the economic consequences of a pandemic can help minimize the impact that the virus has. It can also aid in helping you remain sane during the pandemic.

Closing businesses during the period of self-isolation, which normally lasts for 14 days or more, will doubtlessly have a toll on the economy. Nonetheless, preparing in advance for the negative economic and psychological impact will help in recovering more rapidly.

TAKING AND IMPLEMENTING BUSINESS ADVICE FROM EXPERTS HELPS KEEP YOUR BUSINESS AFLOAT

One major concern that most businesses and freelancers have during a pandemic is how to keep business processes flowing. Fortunately, there are steps that you can take to continue operating your business or even venture into new business ideas. Expert advice can help you retain your sanity and keep your business going in a pandemic. Expert billionaire entrepreneurs are offering their expert advice on social media.

Billionaire entrepreneur Mark Cuban for example has given valuable business advice on LinkedIn. You can go ahead and check it out. Mark Cuban provides some of the tips for keeping your professional life going. These include:

- Reaching out to potential clients as well as trying new business ideas.
- If you cannot carry out some of the work you do at the office while at home you can always try getting a new job by finding potential clients or opportunities.
- You can also start perfecting work or working on neglected work as well as unfinished work.

The billionaire entrepreneur also advises that you try out new ideas, for example, begin offering other services apart from the leading service you provide if you can.

PREPARE FOR A BUSINESS CONTINUITY PLAN

Since my early years of being a Change Management Consultant (specializing in BPR, Business Process Re-Engineering) back in the 1980's, I have worked with numerous corporations in guiding their management team and employees through time of crisis. Preparing an emergency plan for your organization and business can make a huge difference in your company's ability to recover from a disaster. Businesses should adopt simple survival model: Prevention, Preparedness, Forward Thinking, Sustainability.

The goal of Business Continuity Plan:

- to prepare you to **react** and **respond** to unpredicted incidents and keeps your business operations going
- to safeguard your business operations

"Your Business Continuity Plan should be part of the VEIN to your business life." Nicky Dare

It is of utmost importance that a business puts in place a risk management committee consisting of experts in various fields (IT, security, Human resource, Finance etc..) which will identify key personnel and allocate specific tasks during a pandemic. A pandemic planning and coordination must be thoroughly prepared. It must identify the various risk elements which the pandemic will pose against the business. This could include human resource risks, supply chain risks, IT risks, process risks, economic risks etc.

Once a plan is set up, it must be tested and rehearsed regularly. Staff training and educational workshop must be conducted to ensure that everyone in the business knows his duty and responsibility when such event happens. The heart of the business in such instance would be the IT infrastructure which should be robust enough to allow for staff to work from home, while maintaining a secure environment to prevent data breaches or communication down time.

Here are some creative and fun ways to help you and your family stay connected, entertained, and productive during the lockdown.

More Fun and Creative Resources During a Pandemic

Stuck at home during a pandemic? Try these 10 activities to avoid getting crazy!

When authorities declare a Pandemic situation, you, like the rest of the world, are home-bound to mitigate the propagation of the disease. Staying at home is enjoyable for the first few days, but staying on lockdown for many days can drive anyone crazy. The best way to avoid getting out of your mind during a pandemic is to have things to do.

Here is a lot of some exciting activities you can try out if you have to stay at home:

1. Clean up or revamp your house

Staying at home is an opportunity to declutter, clean up, and reorganize your house. You have all the time you have always needed, why not use it to improve your home? A clean and tidy house will also make it enjoyable to stay indoors during quarantine and also to do some work from home. You can take a step further and redecorate the living room and maybe even repaint the bedrooms if you have that kind of resources. To enjoy revamping your house, even more, look for original inspiration online, watch home deco videos on YouTube, and read some blogs.

2. Make a list of things you have always wanted to do

Many people have something they have always wanted to do but never found the time. If you are stuck at home during a pandemic, you can use the time to get some of those things done. Make a list of everything you have always wanted to do and the time it would take to get each one of them done. Focusing on trying to achieve some of your long-standing objectives can prevent you from going crazy.

3. Take a new course to learn new skills or to improve existing skills

During the pandemic lockdown, you can use some of the extra time to educate yourself by learning new skills or by enhancing some of your current skills. Improving yourself can be very useful in getting ahead after the pandemic when things go back to normal. It is also a perfect way to block out crazy thoughts and feelings of doom that invade the mind during a time of isolation.

4. Get into vlogging and blogging

Prior to this outbreak madness, I just started reigniting my efforts in Vlogging and Blogging since early January. It has helped me in many areas in my own personal development, as much as sharing it all to inspire others. If you are into YouTube videos and reading blogs, you can start your own YouTube channel or create a blog, just like what I did. The contents of your blogging can be anything that you want; The goal is to have fun with it and use it as an outlet to let out steam and keep yourself from going crazy. This will not only help you to be creative, and staying productive but also to boost your motivation while helping others. When you have time, no rush, check out my Vlogs on my YouTube channel: www.YouTube.com/c/NickyDare

Feel free to subscribe and leave me your feedback in any of the videos you have watched.

For my blogging, I had put together some inspirational articles, and resources: www.NickyDare.blogspot.com.

Feel free to leave feedback! Let me know what you think.

5. Do not be afraid to pamper yourself

It is ok to indulge yourself in hard times. Researches show that doing something pleasant for yourself can be very therapeutic. So if you are stuck at home, take some time every other day to pamper yourself. It does not even have to be anything fancy; simple things like taking a bubble bath, surrounding yourself with scented candles can be quiet relaxing and therapeutic.

6. Make plans for future holidays

When you are stuck at home during a pandemic, you do not have to sit around and worry about the crazy events. Instead, you should do things that give you joy and hope. Start planning for your future holidays; Research on possible destinations and activities which you could do at that destination. The positive feeling that comes from planning the next event can be beneficial in avoiding the feelings of doom, which often accompany a pandemic lockdown.

7. Learn a new language

Another exciting activity you could engage in to stop yourself from going crazy during a pandemic is to learn a new language. If you are going to plan a future holiday or trip, why not just go a step further and also learn the local language of the place you intend to visit?

8. Think of new goals

A pandemic will pass, and life will return to normal. Take some time to reflect on your goals, what you have achieved, and what you can do better. Come up with new goals and hit the ground running when things go back to normal.

9. Start a new personal project

Having an ongoing project gives people something to look forward. If you are stuck at home, try to start a new project to provide yourself with some purpose, and stop yourself from going crazy. Craft projects, genealogical tree, pot planting are just a few ideas. Be original in your imagination; you may surprise yourself!

10. Rediscover old forgotten games and TV shows

Being stuck at home is also an excellent opportunity to catch up on some TV shows and rediscover some old and forgotten games that you were once watching or playing. If you are at home with your family you could revisit some classic board games.

10 CREATIVE WAYS TO ENTERTAIN YOUR KIDS DURING A PANDEMIC

During a pandemic, everyone is affected irrespective of gender or age. People of all walks of life are affected and kids are not spared. By their very nature, kids are hyperactive- they need to move, they need to interact and focus on specific activities. Not being able to go to school, play with other kids or just run outside can have a lasting impact in their lives. It is every parent's and guardian's responsibility to minimize the negative impact of the lock down on children. Doing this requires a certain level of creativity throughout the duration of the lockdown.

1. Play fun group games

There are quite a number of board games that your kids can play to stay distracted during a pandemic. The most important thing to keep in mind is to stick to the kind of games that they love. You can also take part in some of the games to make things more interesting. You could pick the game once in a while but involve the kids in the selection of a game and stress to them that selecting a game is their responsibility.

2. Play brain stimulating games

Brain games or games that challenge the intellect will not only keep your kids mentally sharp, but it will also keep them competitive and entertained. Compliment your children when they complete a level or stage to keep them motivated and feeling proud. Encourage them when they fail to complete a certain level the same way you would encourage them when they are doing their homework.

3. Try online games

You can also try playing online games with your kids or let them play with their friends online. However, keep a close eye on the kind of games and activities they choose to play online.

4. Let your kids help with the household chores

Household chores are yet another activity, aside of games, you can engage with your kids. Teach them or ask them to give you a hand with the chores and make it interesting. They can help prepare their favorite meal, help set the table, and help clean the house by dusting the furniture. They can also help with washing or folding the laundry. Some kids love it when they do something that their parents encourage or ask them to do. So, give it a try!

5. Start a family project

You can come up with certain family projects that your kids can participate in. It could be any type of project that your kids will love. It does not have to be a school project. It could be the kind of project that they can actively contribute to. For example, you can grow pot-based plants, repaint the bedrooms or build a 3D puzzle or create your genealogical tree. You could even learn a family dance on YouTube or form a band if you have instruments laying around.

6. Give them books to read

Books are a great way of keeping your kids' minds off the pandemic. So, try giving them books to read. You could give every child a different book according to their age and then ask for a 5-minute summary every day before they go to bed. This will not only keep them busy, but it will also perfect their intellect as well as feed their curiosity. Make sure there is a reward for each completed book.

7. Help with their schoolwork

While kids are asked to stay at home while schools are closed, they may be given assignments and homework. You can keep your kids entertained by helping them out with their homework. If the school does not give them any work to do while at home, you can come up with your own assignments. Focus on areas that your child is currently struggling with at school so as to help make the work comprehensible.

8. Watch movies with them

Movies are without a doubt a great source of entertainment for both adults and kids. You could watch one or two movies a day with your kids as a form of entertainment.

9. Have them come up with their own ideas of entertainment

Coming up with great ideas of entertainment for your kids is a good thing. Nonetheless, if you want them to truly enjoy you can let them come up with their own forms of entertainment. Doing so is also a great way to empower them when you have run out of ideas. All you have to do is approve of the kind of entertainment they choose and participate cheerfully when asked.

10. Help cultivate their talents

It is true that every dark cloud has a silver lining. Even during a pandemic your kids' talent can be improved. You can take advantage of the situation and find ways of improving or even discovering your child's talent. For example, if your child is an aspiring artist encourage the artist in him or her by buying color books, pencils, and crayons. You could also go the extra mile by visiting reputable art galleries online and explaining what each photo symbolizes, where and when the painting was made, and what inspired the artist to produce that particular painting.

10 CREATIVE & FUN FAMILY ACTIVITIES YOU CAN DO AT HOME

Being stuck at home as a family can sometimes get boring, especially if you always stick to the same tried and tested activities like watching movies and playing monopoly. The things you do at home with your family often condition the amount and quality of fun you will experience. If you have an abnormally long amount of time to spend at home with your family, you have to be creative and try new exciting activities.

Here are some fun and innovative ideas to boost your family time:

1. Origami

Origami is an ancient Japanese art that involves folding paper to make different kinds of shapes like animals, plants, etc. It is an engaging form of art that anyone can learn. To learn origami, all you need is some white paper, color pencils, scissors and glue. You can easily follow tutorials on YouTube together as a family. Depending on how competitive your family members are, you can also have Origami contests after you have mastered several shapes.

Recently some artists have gone on to add some led lights to the paper shapes to give the artwork some beautiful light and color scenery. To kick things up a notch, add colored led lights and display the forms in the house.

2. Indoor camping

Indoor camping is another fun activity for families. It is easy to set up, and everything you need is usually already available in the house. You can turn the living room into a camp out space, turn off the lights, and take turns telling scary stories while roasting marshmallows on a portable burner.

3. Make short movies

Depending on how many you are in your family, you could write and create short video clips that you record using a phone or a camcorder if you have one. The idea is to have everyone participate in the whole movie-making process, including writing the script, picking the wardrobe, and acting it out. Keep the dialogue short so that you do not have to memorize a lot of words. It is even more fun if you turn the whole house into a movie set.

4. Treasure hunt

A treasure hunt is another way of having fun as a family. To make it enjoyable, have one person set up the hunting clues and divide the rest of the family into groups. The hunting clues should cater to all different age groups of the family so everyone can actively participate.

5. Indoor Olympics

Organize your own indoor Olympics as an entertainment for goofy and hyperactive family members. Create ten competitions that you can do indoors. The activities have to vary in nature and difficulty so that everyone can enjoy and participate. Assign points according to ranking at the end of each event. The winner of the tournament is the one with the most points at the end of all activities. Ideas for activities include eating competition, cup golf, bucket ball, song lyrics, etc.

6. Family Master Chef

Depending on the resources you have in the house, another very fun activity you can engage in is a cook-off. Just like the TV Master Chef, divide into teams and compete in creating an entirely new dish using a chosen set of ingredients. To make it more interesting, write down the different ingredients on a spin wheel and take turns to spin the wheel to select the ingredients. Use only the selected ingredients for the cook-off!

7. Family Project

Starting a family project is an excellent idea if you are going to spend a considerable number of days at home together as a family. The choice of a project depends on the family's interest, but they can range from redecorating the house to making dress up or superhero costumes together. You can also start a family garden if you have space.

8. Learn a new language

Learning a new language is a fun activity to engage every member of the family. Since it is a new language, everyone will be at par and can start together. Just agree on the language and get it going. There are so many learning apps and free online tutorials available that you cannot miss this opportunity! To get things more exciting, plan a future trip to a country that new language is spoken!

9. Turn your home into an Art Gallery

Get the inner artist out of every family member by organizing a home art festival. Everyone must participate and use his creativity and imagination to express his artistic side by painting, drawing, googling or making collage with old newspapers. At the end, stick all the masterpieces on the walls to create your own family art gallery!

10. Revamp you family photo album

Remove the "digital" dust from your old photos kept on your computer and start a fresh family photo album. This can be a fun activity to do with the family as each family member reminisces the good old souvenirs. Revamping your digital photos will also be a good opportunity to clear up duplicates and irrelevant pictures, freeing up valuable space on your computer or cloud storage.

10 DAILY HOME WORKOUT HABITS DURING A PANDEMIC

Daily routines are super important and may affect your mindset, your outlook in life. A pandemic unquestionably affects your day to day routine, which means there are certain things that you are expected to do and are unable to do. In short, learning to adjust is something you need to do to get through the pandemic. One of the major concerns you may have during a pandemic is the fact that you are no longer able to go to the gym due to prevailing lockdown for your own protection.

Apart from being confined indoors, your health and fitness center may be temporarily closed due to the pandemic. The good news is that you can still attain your targeted gym work out results from just working out from home.

Here are some 10 workout habits you can start today:

1. Set a daily reminder
Working out from home can be a disheartening task especially if you are used to the electric atmosphere of the gym. That is why it is important to come up with effective ways of sticking to your exercise routine regardless of where you are. You can still stay motivated to exercise during a lockdown. Start by setting a daily reminder and staying true to it. You can start the day off with a 20-minute exercise. This is a great way of remaining focused for the rest of the day.

2. Join and follow an online workout program
There are specific exercises that are limited to the gym and are impossible to try out at home. For example, the kind of exercises that require lifting weights, machines etc. If you do not have the right equipment to carry out weight-lifting exercises you can try other forms of free weight exercise. There are many free apps and websites that can teach you alternative home-based exercises that can be easily carried out with no equipment or even websites which show you how to make your own home equipment using materials available at hand.

3. Continue with some of the exercises that you do at the gym
While some exercises you do at the gym are impossible to do at home, there are still a few that you can continue doing from home. Continuing with some of your gym exercises from home can help keep you motivated to exercise. It is also a great way of forming a lasting workout habit.

4. Keep a record of your progress

Keeping a record of what you have achieved or what you are achieving will assist in keeping you focused. You could record your weight the first day you begin exercising and keep a log as you continue with your workout routine. Losing weight can make you realize just how effective exercising from home is and hopefully keep you at it.

5. Avoid exercising alone whenever possible

Accountability is another way of ensuring you do what you plan to do. Find someone you can exercise with at home and hold each other accountable. You can set goals or commit to exercising daily for an hour or so. It will all depend on what you both agree on and what you can do. If you have no one to workout with at home, you can find workout buddies online or using workout phone apps.

6. Have a variety of exercises

Varying exercises can help keep you interested in the workout schedule. It can also get rid of the boredom that you may otherwise face if you remain idle.

7. Make working out a priority

Making sure you stick to your workout schedule in a pandemic requires that you make working out a priority. We all have top priorities and staying safe during a pandemic is one of them, therefore, exercising routinely should also top the list.

8. Pay attention to your diet

Paying attention to your diet is the only way of enjoying the full benefits that working out offers. Make sure your exercise routine goes together with proper meals and avoid junk snacking which is tempting when idle at home.

9. Reward yourself

Make sure you reward yourself whenever you manage to stay true to your goal. Small rewards can be a great way of not only keeping you determined to exercise but they can also aid in helping you maintain the positivity that you need during a pandemic.

10. Put on proper workout attire

When working out from home it is important that you wear proper workout attire. What you wear should be the same attire that you would wear when going out to a proper gym. Wearing proper workout gear will tune your mind to that activity and make you feel, and experience exercise the same way you would in a normal gym.

10 TIPS FOR AGING PERSONS DURING A PANDEMIC

Older people face a higher risk of getting infected during a pandemic because they may have weaker immune systems, making them more susceptible to illnesses. Elderlies with chronic illnesses are exposed to a higher risk.

It is crucial to be aware of the best ways of looking out for them.

Here are other means of protecting you during a pandemic, if you form part of this more vulnerable group:

1. Continue taking vitamin supplements

You must continue to take vitamin supplements to support a healthy immune system. Hence, it is wise to keep up with your supplements to help your body fight infections more effectively.

If you are not taking any supplements, you can get in touch with your health advisor to find out if you can start, especially if you have any chronic illnesses. Some of the supplements recommended are vitamin B12, calcium, and vitamin D. it is essential to bear in mind that not all supplements aid in supporting a healthy immune system.

2. Continue taking your medications

You must continue your medication while quarantined. Therefore, make sure you have your regular medication readily available or well-stocked. You can talk to a health professional about having access to 2 months of medicines during isolation. If you are living with other people, you can speak to them about your need to stock up on medical supplies as well.

3. Thoroughly wash your hands

Washing your hands thoroughly or staying sanitized while you stay at home can never be overemphasized. Wash your hands thoroughly with soap and, ideally, warm water using the 20 seconds rule. Use antibacterial hand sanitizers and avoid touching your face, nose, and mouth. Keep your home and frequently touched surfaces disinfected.

4. Maintain a healthy diet

Being in isolation does not mean you have to worry about not eating healthy. Making eating a healthy diet one of your priorities is advisable. Focus on foods that aid in boosting your immune system and foods that can protect you from infections and harmful viruses. Limit or avoid sugary foods, fatty foods, and alcohol. Focus on diets rich in lean meats as well as fruits and vegetables etc. Increase your intake of food rich in antioxidants, which help protect your cells from damage.

5. Avoid sharing personal items

Avoid sharing personal or hygiene items such as utensils, water bottles, food, and bathing soap with others. This small reflex can play a significant role in protecting you and your loved ones from getting infected or spreading the infection.

6. Get enough sleep

Getting plenty of rest is a compelling way of staying healthy and reducing your stress levels. Make sure you not only get enough sleep every night but that you get enough rest throughout the day. One of the significant reasons you may be more vulnerable to illnesses during a pandemic is due to too much stress and not getting enough rest. So make sure you reduce your stress levels by getting enough sleep, proper rest, and remaining active.

7. Remain active

Staying healthy and remaining active does not necessarily require you to go out. You can continue improving your health even if you have to stay at home by being active every day. Moving around and getting active plays a significant role in helping your body fight off infections and inflammation. You can stay active by doing non-strenuous exercises such as doing household chores. You can also try meditation as well as stretching exercises if this is possible. However, you must avoid exercising for more than an hour a day to prevent fatigue.

8. Keep in touch with your caregiver

A lot of older people have caregivers, and some are caregivers. If you have a caregiver and he or she cannot afford to come over to your house, you can keep in touch via calls or messaging. Talk to your caregiver about who can provide you with care if he or she falls ill. If you are a caregiver, you need to make sure that you and the person you are caring for take the necessary precautions to avoid getting infected.

9. Stay at home

Understand that the advice to stay at home during a pandemic is good advice that is for your benefit. If you are not infected, stay at home as you are more vulnerable to getting infected. If you are concerned about groceries, you can do online shopping or ask a family member to do your groceries. Contact a health professional if you have a persistent dry cough and a high fever.

10. Avoid large groups

If you are at a residential care home, make sure you avoid large groups. If you have a large family, make sure you keep a safe distance from others and avoid shaking hands or close physical contact.

10 THINGS TO AVOID WHEN QUARANTINED DURING PANDEMIC

A quarantine for a majority of us, an unprecedented experience. In such situation, there are a lot of unknown and often unanswered questions. It is essential, however, to know what you can do and what you cannot. This article will address the 10 main things you need to avoid when quarantined. Here are some critical things to be aware of:

1. Avoid contact with other people

If you need to self-quarantine, you have to isolate yourself from others. Protect others from getting infected by keeping your distance and avoid being in the same room with them, as far as possible. Depending on how the infection in question is transmitted, do not share dishes, towels, eating utensils, bedding items, and other personal items with other people.

Adopting these habits will help control and prevent further infections. Clean all surfaces and frequently manipulated devices such as computers and mobile phones using a disinfectant. Always remain alert to symptoms related to that particular infection.

2. Do not entertain visitors

Avoid the risk of spreading the infection if you have been quarantined by stopping social visits and other close contacts. You can order takeaways, but make sure you avoid physical contact with the person delivering the order. Protect people who help out with house chores by requesting them not to come to work, at least during the quarantine period. Such people may include child-minders, housekeepers and dog walkers.

3. Avoid contact with your pet

Your pet can unknowingly become a transmitter of viruses. Limiting contact with your pets when quarantined is a way of protecting yourself as well as your pet. Avoid getting licked by your pet, petting your pet, as well as sharing food with your pet. If possible, ask someone else to be responsible for with your pet while in quarantine.

4. Avoid traveling

It is safer to refrain from moving outside for whatsoever reason while in quarantine. Make sure you stay at home and avoid spreading the infection to others. If your symptoms start worsening, make sure you call your doctor first and avoid showing up without any warning. Alternatively, head to the medical facility where they have set up a specialized zone for such pandemic-related symptoms.

5. Avoid coughing or sneezing without covering your mouth or nose

If transmission of the virus is via droplets, cover your mouth and nose when coughing or sneezing to help contain and prevent the spread of infections. Throw away used tissues and wash your hands thoroughly after sneezing or coughing, applying the 20 seconds rule. Wash your hands thoroughly using soap and warm water after going to the bathroom and avoid touching your face, mouth, or nose.

6. Avoid handling food without washing

Always wash your hands before preparing or eating food. Avoid preparing food for others while quarantined to prevent the spread of the infection if you show some symptoms of infection.

7. Do not leave your health to chance

Avoid relying on other people for knowledge of how you can best take care of yourself as well as your loved ones while quarantined. Make sure you are well aware of what you must do once you or a loved one are self-isolating. Have proper knowledge of the steps that need to be taken and know what to buy. Make sure you have access to all the necessary items needed while quarantined. Do not hesitate to contact health professionals when the symptoms start worsening.

8. Avoid assuming your kids understand what is happening

Being quarantined or being in self-isolation can cause a lot of discomfort to your loved ones. Make sure you educate your kids about pandemics and quarantines. Make sure they understand that being quarantined does not mean the presence of an infection. Calmly explain to them the situation and the reason for staying at home. Educate them on the precautions to take during that time.

9. Avoid disconnecting with your loved ones completely

Avoiding physical contact with your loved ones does not mean to be emotionally or socially disconnected. You are also encouraged to keep in touch using emails, calls, or social media. Maintaining this virtual contact will significantly reduce stress levels.

10. Avoid self-medicating

One mistake people make when quarantined is trying to control or get rid of the first symptoms by self-medicating. Do not self-medicate or increase dosages if you are already under specific medication. Self-medication or the risk of overdosing will not help you fight or prevent suspected infections.

10 TIPS TO STAY POSITIVE WHEN EVERYONE AROUND IS GOING CRAZY (...seriously!)

Staying positive when the world is going crazy is one of the best ways of surviving the tide and making it out of the storm. However, this task can be challenging but may possibly be the only thing which can get you out of the woods. It requires a strong mindset for me, it is either taking care of yourself, self care, or occupying my time with exciting projects, small or big.

. If you are struggling to bring yourself to remain positive in times of calamity, here are some tips to help you:

1. Plan ahead

I am all about this - "Be Prepared"! Planning ahead can help control your stress levels and anxiety in a world where people are going crazy. That is one way of knowing you can face anything. One way of making sure you and your loved ones remain positive when faced with negativity is by being well prepared for whatever comes. That is why it is advisable to be prepared for emergencies before they occur. You can prepare for a pandemic before it strikes. You can achieve this by taking the necessary measures needed before it begins-Adequate food, reinforced shelter, warm clothing etc., relevant equipment etc.

2. Filter information

Avoid bad news whenever you can. Do not focus on the kind of information that will not help rectify the situation. Pay attention to material that gives advice on how you can overcome or guard against being affected by the worsening of the pandemic. Filtering information can also mean changing the subject when it is brought up countless times.

3. Keep exercising

As you know, exercising is a great way of staying positive, staying healthy, and improving your overall physical and mental well-being. Exercising can also help keep your mind in check. Concentrating on improving your health is another method of staying positive when everyone else is going insane. One mistake you can make when faced with difficulties is changing or cancelling your workout routine. Therefore, keep exercising and enjoy the process.

4. Dwell on happy thoughts

Thinking happy thoughts does not come easy when it seems as if your world is falling apart. That is why you have to try and force your mind to focus on happy thoughts or what is happening internally and not externally. If you cannot think of anything that shifts your mind from the bad news that is being broadcasted everywhere, create happy thoughts. You can achieve this by envisioning where you will be when all the madness is over. Think about the number of people who have overcome or who are overcoming the same situation you are in, look at your photo album and rekindle the happy memories.

5. Manage your finances

Mishandling your finances is quite easy when you are dealing with a pandemic or a problem that affects a lot of people at the same time. Hence, you need to start managing your finances wisely to avoid having regrets when the problem has passed. You can avoid bankruptcy by just staying calm, avoiding compulsive debts and keeping accurate records and information.

6. Try caring for someone else

Sometimes caring for someone else is all it takes to maintain your sanity. Shift your focus to doing something worthwhile for someone else or putting a smile on someone else's face. Achieve this by helping the person you choose to help or care for stay safe or recover from what they are going through.

7. Meditate

Meditation is an excellent way of relaxing your mind and having a much clearer perspective on things. Meditation is a relaxation method that you can begin practicing right away. If it is something that you are practicing already, continuing with it is worthwhile. Try clearing your mind from negative thoughts and focus on one thing that is positive. Do this every single day for at least 30 minutes without any interruptions.

8. Continue with your work or studies

You may start panicking if you think that your professional life is on hold during a pandemic. However, realize that not being able to go to the office does not necessarily mean the end of progress- this will help you remain calm. Continue with your work or study even if you cannot go to the office or on campus. Remember that working or studying from home has its fair share of benefits as well. You are able to work peacefully without the worries of dressing up, with zero or a few distractions. You are able to control your environment and work at your own pace.

9. Enjoy whatever you do

Make it a priority to enjoy whatever you do during the pandemic. If you are working on something that you have to do but not necessarily enjoy, try coming up with fun or alternative ways of doing things. Instead of doing your work or completing your projects the way your supervisor suggests, you can do it your own creative way, as long as the job done impeccably and impressively.

10. Avoid negative people

No matter what happens in the world, negative people will always look for ways to blow things out of proportion. That is why avoiding negative people in supposedly perilous times is the best thing to do. If you are told to stay at home and cannot avoid those sharing the house, you can encourage the people around you to remain positive. While it may be impossible to make sure everyone stays positive, you can always bring up something positive to talk about. This will change the atmosphere.

Have the right reflexes when self-isolating

An infection outbreak is a stressful time that often requires the adoption of stringent but necessary measures. During a pandemic, people are forced to self-isolate to curb the spread of the disease and prevent new infections. It is a critical aspect of mitigating the disease, and as such, everyone should play their role adequately.

Self-isolation has two objectives: To protect yourself and to protect others. Knowing how to behave and act when one is alone or when they are amongst other people is essential. Therefore, you need to develop the right attitude and reflexes when self-isolating.

To protect yourself and the people around you, here are some behavioral do's and don'ts that should be on the tip of your fingers:

Always act to limit contact

Self-isolation limits contact with other people, save for those with whom you are in self-isolation. Whatever you do, it should be on the top of your mind to avoid contact or physical meetings with other people, infected or not. Avoid having visitors in your house. Do not visit other people. Do not go out unless necessary, and even then, make sure you take precautions to protect yourself and to protect other people.

Self-monitoring is key

Always monitor yourself for the signs and symptoms of the disease. These signs can be early symptoms of the disease or symptoms of the infection worsening. Use a reliable source to educate yourself on the signs and symptoms to consider.

Hygiene, sanitation, and more Hygiene

Being in self-isolation does not mean that you do not have to follow the hygiene recommendations issued by the health authorities. Continue to practice personal hygiene and surface sanitation when you are in self-isolation. Make it a point to disinfect all surfaces and points of frequent contact after each use, especially if you are living with other people.

Think of vulnerable individuals

Whatever you do during self-isolation, always think of vulnerable individuals around you. Susceptible groups include people at the extreme ends of age and people suffering from chronic and pre-existing conditions like diabetes, asthma, etc. Think of these people and try to put them first in everything you do during self-isolation, whether diagnosed with the infection or not.

Seek help when needed

You should not hesitate to ask your healthcare provider for help if you have any problem or you are not sure about something. Self-isolation does not mean you should figure things out on your own. If you develop a symptom, before you decide to self-medicate, ask someone else with authority and knowledge for advice and confirmation.

Stay informed

Make it a habit to always stay informed. Follow news updates on the outbreak and go beyond by reading scientific articles related to the outbreak. The more you know about the disease, the better you will be equipped to help fight it. One thing though, always ensure that your sources are reliable as lousy information is worse than no information.

Think Positive

While it is essential to stay informed about the progress of the pandemic, you should not let the news of growing number of cases or even deaths impact you negatively. Remember that bad news always sells very well. Do not get in their game. Be informed but do not be influenced by what you hear. Always keep a positive outlook on things and find ways to distract yourself.

Get fit

When self-isolating, it is always tempting to laze yourself on the couch in front of the TV. While this may be fine for the first days, remember that self-isolation could last for a few weeks. So, keeping fit physically will not only help your body but also your state of mind. Do some stretching exercise or some light exercise. There are ample of fitness programs available online with varying degrees of difficulty.

10 HEALTH HABITS TO BOOST YOUR IMMUNE SYSTEM

In a pandemic that mostly affects people with immunity problems it is always best to take some measure to boost your immune system, mental and physical health in general. Here are some useful ways of boosting your immune system and preventing illness:

1. Make nutrition a priority.

Making nutrition a priority is something that you need to constantly pay attention to. Eating healthy without panic buying during a pandemic is possible. You only need to focus on food that you normally eat especially if you are already eating well. If you are not, then you can start doing so and avoid overstocking on high carb food. Making nutrition a priority during a pandemic means making sure everyone in the house eats healthy by having a balanced diet.

2. Buy nutrient-rich foods.

Nutrient-rich foods such as beans or lentils, whole wheat foods, and foods high in fiber should be on your grocery list. The best thing about such foods is that they can be prepared in various ways and they can be mixed with other foods. You not only enjoy your meal, but you get the complete nutritional benefits as well.

3. Eat more fruits and vegetables.

Fruits and vegetables are excellent sources of high-nutrient foods that will keep you healthy during a pandemic. There are many concerns that may arise when it comes to best ways of consuming your fruits and vegetables, such as safe ways of washing and preparing them. Nonetheless, this is not something that you need to worry too much about. Experts say that there is no need to panic. Continue washing your fruits and vegetables the same way you always do. There is no need for using sanitizers to wash your fruits and vegetables like most people assume.

4. Stay Hydrated

Drinking lots of water will keep your body hydrated and will drain any accumulatio of bacteria or viruses in your mouth or throat. Avoid drinking sugared or soda drinks- the sugar will only contribute in dehydrating your body.

5. Maintain a good hygiene

Washing your hands thoroughly or staying clean is a great way of ensuring perfect health. You are advised to wash your hands for 20 seconds with soap or using an alcohol-based sanitizer. Staying clean also involves focusing on keeping your house clean and getting rid of clutter. Make sure you emphasize cleanliness to your kids and help them clean up. Let them tidy up their rooms and arrange their toys every night before going to bed.

6. Avoid physical contact or touching your face

Health professionals advise that you should avoid touching your face during an infection outbreak. This is because touching your face can lead to major infections or the spread of viruses and bacteria which can affect your immune system. Minimize contact with others as well to prevent risks of contamination.

7. Home workouts.

Exercising from home is also a great way of staying healthy during an outbreak. When your physical body is fit, the mind is also fit, and this plays a huge role in your ability to stay healthy even during the most menacing outbreaks. Remember to stay hydrated throughout your exercise routine.

8. Get quality sleep

Amid the constant negative news around, people tend to stay awake, worrying or watching the development of the pandemic. Remember that sleep is essential to help the body restore and regenerate itself. So try to sleep at a decent time with at least 7 hours of good quality sleep. You will wake up feeling rested and to face the challenging day.

9. Natural supplements

Natural supplements have proved time and time again to be effective in boosting the immune system. Natural supplements like ginger, essential oils, lavender, coriander and more have proven healing and immunity boosting properties. Vitamins also help to supplement the body's daily vitamins and minerals intake and prevent you from easily catching infection and falling ill.

10. Keep track of your health

Another way to stay on top of your immunity is by tracking your vital health signs. Following simple things like body temperature, blood pressure and glucose levels can help you stay on top of the situation and seek care on time instead of waiting until you have been affected by an infection.

10 TIPS TO STAY HEALTHY WHILE YOU ARE STUCK AT HOME

Being on lockdown during a pandemic should not be an excuse to let go of your body and engage in an unhealthy lifestyle. If you have to stay indoors longer than usual, it is even more essential to adopt a healthy lifestyle. In that way, you can avoid putting yourself at risk for certain conditions linked to unhealthy living. By staying on top of your behavior when you are stuck at home, you can prevent yourself from developing things like diabetes, high blood pressure, obesity, and muscle atrophy. Studies have shown that people who do not maintain a healthy lifestyle when stuck at home often find it difficult to resume normal activities after the home period is over. Going back to work may prove challenging. So if you are going to be held at home, for whatever reason, here are some tips to help you stay healthy:

1. Eat healthily

You would think that this tip does not require mentioning, but you will be surprised at the things people eat when they are stuck at home. It's fine to eat junk food once in a while, but going on a junk food bender during a lockdown can cause you many issues. So take some time and plan out your meals and snacks. For every 90% of whole, healthy foods, you can reward yourself with 10% of feel-good fare.

2. Get physical

Most people mistake physical exercise for body looks. It's much more than that, exercise helps the body release stress, clear the mind, and it is good for the heart as it gets the blood flowing. When you are stuck at home, exercising can boost your sense of wellbeing and prevent you from suffering from dangerous health conditions like depression and anxiety.

3. Read books

With online streaming sites being so popular, it is easy to get stuck on the couch and binge-watch tv shows. However, people tend to forget the negative impact of long hours watching tv on the eyes, back, and intellect. In order to stay healthy when you are stuck indoors try and incorporate some books in between your tv shows. Taking time off the screen and moving images can do you a lot of good in as far as your eyes are concerned. Audiobooks can also help with the advantage of doing another activity while listening to the book.

4. Feed the mind

Maintaining some level of intellect is another way of staying healthy when stuck at home. There are many ways of keeping your brain active during a lockdown. You could play strategy and logic games that require you to think. You could also enroll in an online course or join forums that discuss highly intellectual topics.

5. Take care of your mental health

When one is stuck indoors, they risk developing mental health issues, especially if they are alone. Taking care of your mental health is an absolute priority when you are locked down. You need to maintain contact with friends and family if you are going to be stuck indoors for a long time. You do not necessarily need it to be physical contact, video chats, texting, and phone calls can do just fine.

6. Find a project

Having a sense of purpose can play a crucial role in maintaining a healthy attitude when stuck at home. It does not even have to be a big project. Just a simple project with results can work wonders. You can embark on a simple project like redecorating your room or something a bit more challenging, like DIY (Do-It-Yourself) projects.

7. Improve yourself

When you are stuck at home, you could use that time to improve yourself. Learn a new skill that will help you get ahead when you eventually return to the world. Educating yourself will remove the unhealthy feeling of being "stuck" and replace it with feelings of finding a new purpose.

8. Help others

Being helpful to other people while you are stuck at home can do wonders for your mental health. There are many ways of helping other people that you can try. One example would be to help older people do online shopping. Another example would be to take some time to listen to other people's problems (although not too much to avoid being depressed yourself). You can dispense services directly linked to your profession, which can also help you stay fresh and sharp for when you eventually return to your work.

9. Explore and expand your horizons

It is always healthy to explore and expand one's horizons. The world has so much more to offer than what you already know or think. So when stuck at home, take time to explore other cultures, try new foods, and above all, make sure you come out on the other side a better and stronger person.

10. Do not miss your medical consultations

Lastly, if you have medical conditions or scheduled checkups, do not pass upon them. Instead, use technology to turn up for your medical appointments and consultations. If you have prescriptions to renew, you can also do that using telemedicine platforms and other technology.

Helpful Resources and Support:

https://www.Education.NickyDare.com
https://www.NickyDare.com

Books and Courses

Dare's Guide To Combat Your Stress in a Chaotic World | 10-week eCourse Roadmap to guide you find your inner peace

4-week Challenge in Developing Your Productivity Habits and Self Discipline

Dare's Virtual Network

These are challenging times filled with uncertainties. You do not have to go through this all alone. Nicky Dare, the host, is creating a support group, a place for you, for anyone and everyone to:

- share your challenges, obstacles, and yes also wins!
- build relationships with other fellow business owners
- improve your problem-solving abilities in a group / team
- get a sense of belonging and fun (yes we wear funny hats when speaking!) while working remotely
- a place where you can share and offer ideas and solutions to one another
- if you just want to hang out with us, we love to have you too!

Feel free to join us, and learn more: www.NickyDare.com/ StayHome

Your feedback is a gift!

If you have reached to this page: thank you!

I would love to hear your thoughts, and feedback after you read this guide.

If you wish, please leave your review on the amazon page, or email us: books@nickydare.com, or directly to me: hello@nickydare.com.

Thank you so very much in advance.

I hope you enjoy this easy-to-read guide to help you and your family and loved ones during this uncertain time. Let us all continue to share OPTIMISM, KINDNESS, and LOVE around the world. From my home to yours.

We are all in this together.

Stay vigilant, and stay safe!

Nicky Dare

Ms. Dare is an outdoor enthusiast whose life journey has been part of fulfilling her personal development. In the last decade, Dare has been helping people to prepare and get trained for the worst and unexpected disasters, both in natural and man made. As an educator, Dare is passionate helping individuals, families, and groups train and prepare mentally, physically, and financially.

"People don't like to plan for the worst, but preparedness and knowledge is what separates the survivors from the victims. Disasters and emergencies can strike at any time and most without warning. Even though we may not be 100% prepared, cultivating knowledge and gaining survival mindset and skills can help drastically reduce disaster risks."
Nicky Dare, "Safety and Survival" (2018).

Her hands-on experiences and generous character make for a combination unlike any other. Dare spent most of her lifetime enjoying the outdoors, experiencing the survival wilderness, as well as learning urban survival challenges in different parts of the world. She uses her real-world insights to help educate and train many people and organizations. Dare is widely considered as on the industries most qualified and most experienced professionals. Dare offers a variety of services, including this phenomenal resource, for those who want to develop the necessary skills to keep themselves and their loved ones safe.

In respond to the pandemic outbreak, Dare created a global awareness "30-Day Challenge" #DAREToSaveLives, a cause with its goal to connect people, virtually, around the world to save lives during the unprecedented pandemic by taking part in staying home: staying safe and healthy. To learn more of this amazing cause, go to: https://idarecares.org

Author "Safety and Survival: Personal Preparedness Assessment Guide" (2018) and "The Audacity of Veracity" (2014). More of her books are coming soon.

For more, go to her website: www.NickyDare.com

About The Author

Educator, Author, Founder of iDARE® and DARE Education, President IAW International Association of Women of Santa Clarita Chapter, Corporate Consultant for Change Management and BPR Business Process Re-Engineering, Advocate for Disaster Preparedness, Safety and Survival, most importantly just a prolific human.

Nicky Dare is a seasoned multi-disciplinary professional with extensive experience in business development and strategic planning executive. Her success as a consultant and corporate coach has led her all around the world where she's transformed individuals and businesses alike. Ms. Dare's robust skillset is not merely limited to office settings. She's founded three, yes three, different organizations; Global Meta Management Consultants, Dare Education, and iDARE® Inc. The latter two focuses on personal development in the form of safety preparedness education. As a skilled marksman, Ms. Dare believes that knowledge surrounding emergency preparedness and firearm expertise is paramount. Her non-profit, iDARE® Inc., was born out of a vision from the most powerful mentor in her life; her father. He instilled the importance of living life filled with truth and purpose. Operating off these pillars, iDARE® Inc. is dedicated to helping development communities, empowering women, and educating children that have been impacted by disasters. It is apparent that Ms. Dare's "pillars of excellence" derived from her family values and strong academic and education background including her grandfather who was a prominent figure and reputable District Attorney in Indonesia.

Nicky Dare has a wide range of skills and a deep well of knowledge that she wishes to share with the world. Her book, The Audacity of Veracity, looks at how to create a life filled with health and happiness. This recent publication joins her webinar series on personal development, Safety and Survival: Personal Preparedness Assessment. She's also launched a podcast and does various speaking events, all as a means to share her powerful messages with as many people as possible. A passionate philanthropist, incredible personal life coach, and highly-effective corporate consultant, Ms. Dare truly makes a positive impact on the lives of everyone she meets by helping them to live with a purpose and passion.

She is proud to be a multilingual women's advocate, supporting her community on the committees of various charities and networking organizations. Dare's books and the startup of the iDARE® organization have been fully funded by her late father, who has been the ultimate mentor and inspiration in her life.

Her books are available on Amazon.